Kittens Purr

KINGFISHER

NEW YORK

KINGFISHER
LONDON & NEW YORK

Copyright © Kingfisher 2012
Published in the United States by Kingfisher,
175 Fifth Ave., New York, NY 10010
Kingfisher is an imprint of Macmillan Children's Books, London.
All rights reserved.

Written and designed by Dynamo Ltd.

Distributed in the U.S. and Canada by Macmillan,
175 Fifth Ave., New York, NY 10010

Library of Congress Cataloging-in-Publication data has been applied for.

ISBN 978-0-7534-7002-2

Kingfisher books are available for special promotions and premiums. For details contact:
Special Markets Department, Macmillan, 175 Fifth Ave., New York, NY 10010.

For more information, please visit www.kingfisherbooks.com

Printed in China
9 8 7 6 5 4 3 2 1
1TR/0612/HH/-/140MA

Contents

Which baby hides inside a cozy pouch?

A newborn kangaroo is only the size of a peanut. As soon as it is born, it climbs inside its mother's pouch.

The pouch is safe and warm. Inside, the baby kangaroo drinks its mother's milk and slowly grows bigger.

Baby kangaroos

- A baby kangaroo is called a joey.
- As it grows, the joey starts to hop in and out of the pouch.
- It leaves the pouch for good when it is about eight months old.

A female kangaroo
with her joey

5

Why do kittens purr?

Kittens purr when they are feeling happy. A mother cat purrs at her kittens and licks them to make them feel safe.

When kittens are first born, they cannot see, smell, or hear very well. Their mother's purring lets them know that she is nearby.

Kittens

- Cats give birth to several kittens at once. This is called a litter.

- They are born with their eyes shut and open them after about ten days.

- Kittens drink their mother's milk for about six weeks.

Kittens with their mother

7

Do some babies sleep underground?

Baby rabbits live in burrows under the ground. Their mother builds them a cozy nest using dry grass.

The mother lines the nest with tufts of her own soft fur, and the babies curl up together to stay warm.

Baby rabbits

- A baby rabbit is called a kit.
- Most kits are born in litters with three or four brothers and sisters.
- The kits stay safe in the underground nests while their mothers go off to eat grass.

Baby rabbits in their underground nest

Which baby has a lot of aunts?

Baby elephants live with their mothers in big family groups called herds. Their aunts, grandmothers, brothers, and sisters live with them, too.

Their aunts and grandmothers help take care of them as they grow.

Baby elephants

- A baby elephant is called a calf.
- It drinks its mother's milk until it is big enough to eat grass.
- Male elephants leave the herd when they are about 13 years old.

Baby elephants learn
by copying the older
elephants in the herd

Who hatches from an egg?

Baby birds grow inside eggs. They eat the yolk that is in the egg with them.

Baby birds hatch from their eggs when they are big and strong enough to live outside. They peck their way out through the eggshell and hatch from the egg.

Baby birds

- A baby bird is called a chick.
- Egg white is a thick liquid that protects the chick inside its egg.
- As soon as a chick hatches, it shakes itself to dry its feathers.

Baby birds hatching

Which baby lives on an iceberg?

Baby harp seals are born on frozen sea ice in the far north of the world.

They live on the ice for about eight weeks until they can swim and feed themselves.

Baby harp seals

- Baby seals are called pups.
- The pups drink their mother's milk, which is very thick and creamy.
- The pups have white coats when they are young, but their coats turn gray as they grow.

A baby harp seal
with its mother

Which baby is the biggest?

The baby blue whale is the biggest baby on Earth. When it is born, it weighs about as much as 1,000 human babies.

The baby whale is born underwater. Its mother nudges it to the surface to take its first breath of air.

Baby blue whales

- A baby blue whale is called a calf.
- It is about 25 ft. (7.6m) long when first born. That is roughly as long as a big elephant.
- It will grow 82 ft. (25m) long, about the length of three big elephants standing in a row.

A baby blue whale

Which baby is good at hiding?

A baby deer has a speckled coat that helps it hide in the woods where it is born.

The baby is very hard to see among leaves and bushes, which keeps it safe from animals who would like to eat it.

Baby deer

- A baby deer is called a fawn.
- Mother deer sometimes leave their babies hidden while they go off to feed on grass.
- In some parts of the world, big wild cats or wolves try to catch deer to eat.

18

A baby deer
hiding from a
hungry big cat

19

Who gets carried in its mother's mouth?

A leopard lifts her baby up by gripping the back of its neck with her mouth. All cat mothers can do this.

The baby's skin is loose and baggy behind its neck, so the mother does not hurt it as she gently lifts it up.

Baby leopards

- A baby leopard is called a cub.
- Mother leopards teach their cubs to hunt, climb, and swim.
- Every leopard has its own spotted coat pattern. No two leopards have the same spots.

A mother leopard
carries her baby

21

What do you know about baby animals?

You can find all of the answers to these questions in this book.

Do baby rabbits usually have brothers and sisters?

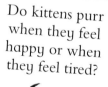

What is a baby deer called?

Do kittens purr when they feel happy or when they feel tired?

How do baby birds get out of their eggs?

Are baby leopards spotted or striped?

Which is your favorite baby animal?

23

Some baby animal words

Burrow A tunnel in the ground where an animal lives.

Hatch To come out of an egg.

Herd A big group of animals that live together.

Litter A group of baby animals born at the same time to the same mother.

Milk A liquid that some animal mothers make to feed their newborn babies.

Nest A soft bed or a shelter made by an animal for its babies.

Pouch A flap of skin, like a pocket, that some female animals have for their babies to hide inside.